Debby

Debby

Deborah Zook

HERALD PRESS
SCOTTDALE, PENNSYLVANIA
KITCHENER, ONTARIO
1974

Library of Congress Cataloging in Publication Data

Zook, Deborah, 1950-
    Debby.

Autobiographical.
1. Blind — Personal narratives. I. Title.
HV1792.Z66A33   362.4'1'0924 [B]   74-5415
ISBN 0-8361-1742-5

DEBBY

Copyright © 1974 by Herald Press, Scottdale, Pa. 15683
Library of Congress Catalog Card Number: 74-5415
International Standard Book Number: 0-8361-1742-5
Printed in the United States

Design by Alice B. Shetler

To my parents
Whose love provided me
With firm footing
And
Whose understanding gave me
Freedom to choose my own path

Contents

PREFACE

Life has so much to offer that it would be foolish to let a little thing like being blind keep one from enjoying it. True living does not depend on the physical conditions surrounding us.

It took me several years and a lot of frustration, confusion, and excitement to learn that I did not need to sit back and let life pass me by. I am grateful for each experience that helped me along the way. I am grateful for the experiences which will occur today, for one never stops learning about living.

The experiences in this book are mine, but excellent help in relating these experiences in a concise and readable form was given by my uncle, Ellrose Zook. His understanding and patience cannot be surpassed. His years of experience in book editing, his belief in the importance of the subject matter of the book, and our friendship combined to provide me with invaluable guidance and help. I could not have done it without him.

Of the many others who made this book possible, I can mention only a few. Rose Marie Combs, a typing student at the vocational school, faithfully and with precision retyped my rough drafts. And I hope my roommate, Myrna Miller, will forgive me for the times I did not do my share of the housework in order to write some more and for the times she was awakened too early in the morning by the sound of typewriter keys.

I hope you find this book interesting reading and much more than that. Perhaps the accounts of how I have learned to live with my handicap will help you cope with some difficult area in your life. Perhaps you will understand better the inner fears and joys of your blind acquaintances. Perhaps you can discover how your life too can become richer and fuller, no matter what obstacles may seem to block that kind of life for you.

Perhaps a look through the eyes of one who is blind can provide you with a renewed and better vision.

Deborah Zook
Hazard, Kentucky

INTRODUCTION

In this book, Debby Zook, a courageous blind girl, reveals her personal experiences which show the physical and psychological barriers encountered in her bid to achieve independence and to retain her individuality. Her book is both entertaining and enlightening. Happily, Debby came, "saw," and conquered the hearts of everyone in Hazard, Kentucky.

Who could blame the people at Hazard Area Vocational-Technical School if they were a bit skeptical at first when Debby Zook arrived to teach the blind? After all, the location and layout of the Vocational School had not been designed to accommodate a blind instructor. Taxi service was the only transportation available to get her to and from school. How would she ever find her way around the school grounds? How could this blind girl find her way around town without someone to lead her?

Hazard was definitely not ready for the educational experiences forthcoming from frail, 22-year-old Debby Zook!

It is no fantasy that Southern people are hospitable. Many well-meaning staff members offered Debby assistance, which she politely but firmly refused. Her somewhat curt "No, thank you; I can manage" often left the "Good Samaritan" standing agape while Debby went about her work with unbelievable poise and self-confidence.

In the two short years Debby has been in Hazard, she has removed skepticism and replaced it with admiration. Her quick smile, sharp wit, and delightful sense of humor are convincing evidence that blindness is no insurmountable obstacle to any desirable goal. She expects and receives no special arrangements for the convenience of herself or the blind students.

Not only is Debby a competent instructor, but she participates in a variety of community functions. She is an active church member, teaches a Sunday school class, belongs to the Business and Professional Women's Club, and is often asked to speak at club meetings or other social events in the Hazard area.

Perhaps there is no such thing as total acceptance of a handicap such as blindness, but Debby is living proof that blind people can be useful, productive citizens who live normal, active lives. Not only has she helped to give great impetus to the hopes of blind people, but her own zest for life is an inspiration to all who are fortunate enough to know her. Possibly her most valuable accomplishment is in helping the sighted to "see."

The author continues to strive for self-improvement. As an indication of her increasing maturity, she now shows little or no sensitivity or discomfort when unsolicited assistance is offered but often gracefully accepts a helping hand she does not necessarily need. Debby Zook can best be described in just three words: *She is beautiful!*

> *Walter Prater, Director*
> *Hazard Regional Vocational Educational Programs*

Debby

Debby

I WAS SITTING alone in the hotel dining room in Louisville, Kentucky. I hoped the waitress would not notice the moistness in my eyes when she asked whether everything was all right with my breakfast. It was, of course. It was, that is, until a strange gentleman startled me with the words that still rang in my ears.

"I just wanted to let you know that I think you're just beautiful," he had said.

How long he had been watching me I had no way of knowing. He left as quickly as he had come. I felt I would never meet him again.

Now I sat toying with my fork. "Just beautiful." The words still rang in my heart.

"God bless that man," I said to myself.

During the first 18 years of my life when I could see,

15

I thought perhaps I was a bit attractive. In fact when I saw my high school portrait, I felt rather sure of it. But with my silver-white cane lying on the floor by my chair and with a few strands of gray hair at the age of 24, I thought surely all that had changed.

Nor did I enjoy being dependent on others, as when the waitress needed to show me to an empty table that morning.

"What is beautiful about being helpless?" I wondered.

I had tried to use my knife and fork carefully as I ate my French toast. But one could not call that beautiful.

Then I remembered the advice of one of my instructors at the Greater Pittsburgh Guild for the Blind in Bridgeville, Pennsylvania, a suburb of Pittsburgh. He had told me that even when I didn't know what was going on, I should respond as though I did. I always tried to appear to have each situation under control even though I was scared to death. But beautiful?

I glided the fork gently across my plate to see whether I had found all the French toast. No, there was one more piece. I moved my right hand slowly toward my juice glass and thoughtfully finished my breakfast. I longed to be able to share my joy with someone, but the closest thing I had to a companion was my cane.

I ARRIVED at the hotel in Louisville the night before after a bus ride from Hazard, Kentucky. The whole trip was special to me. I had come here to get acquainted with an agency that teaches blind people ways of working around the limitations of their blindness. The Rehabilitation Center for the Blind in Louisville was one agency related to my teaching job at Hazard that I needed to know more about. The excitement of making this trip on my own was almost intoxicating.

Before I left Hazard, my friends asked me how I could travel by bus alone. Although I was not really sure myself, I never told them. I called a cab to take me to the bus station at Hazard. On my bus ride to Lexington I busied myself by knitting. At Lexington, I had a short wait for the bus to Louisville.

The bus drivers were especially helpful and accommodating. After I was seated comfortably waiting for the bus to leave, a girl about my age, a student at the University of Kentucky, sat down beside me.

As often happens, I soon discovered that we both shared a strong faith in God. Nothing could have been more reassuring in the middle of an experience in which I was depending, step by step, on God to supply the smallest of my needs.

When I arrived in Louisville, I took a cab to the hotel and checked in. The lady at the desk accompanied me to my room. After she left and the door closed behind her, my heart sang with joy. How I wished I could have shared this experience with someone!

My heart sang, "I made it! I made it! I knew I could do it!"

With my cane I walked cautiously around the room to find the exact location of each piece of furniture. As I passed the place where I thought the radio might be, I reached for it. Yes, there it was. I snapped the knob. Wow! The music that filled the room and my ears seemed to be a message from God, saying, "I'm proud of you, Kid! Real proud!" My heart, still singing, responded, "Thank You, God!"

Between the two double beds stood a night stand. I made a mental note of each piece of furniture as I came to it. When I got back to the door, I walked over to the bed, laid down my cane, and sat down. One deep breath was the closest I could come to expressing my feelings. I kicked off my shoes and felt the rich carpet under my feet.

My minister father, who died when I was 12, would have thought the room extravagant. And it would have been for Father and Mother and their five children, of which I was third. He pastored a mission church along the wooded banks of the Juniata River near the town of Mt. Union among the mountains of central Pennsylvania.

Although we were not rich, we did not consider ourselves deprived. We always had plenty to eat and enough clothing to keep us warm. I remember well the first new dress I received. At eight I could not understand why my mother would not let me keep the tags on. "I wanted everyone to know this one is brand new," I reasoned.

When Mother served cornmeal mush for supper, we kids got the biggest kick out of watching the hunk of butter disappear as the heat of the mush gradually melted it. We ate lots of homemade bread and milk soup. It tasted good. My father was especially fond of it and there was always enough for us to ask for a second or third bowlful.

But candy was more of a rarity in the parsonage. When Mother brought home a bag of M&Ms she

18

carefully divided them into five equal piles. No one thought of eating them at first. M&Ms were good for more than eating. We traded for different colors, built pyramids, and created different designs.

No, this hotel room didn't quite fit into that part of my life.

Then I remembered another room from my past. My room at Juniata College, Huntingdon, Pennsylvania, twelve miles from my home, did not have carpet on the floor. But the furniture was new, with matching desks, and the rooms had built-in closets. After four years at Juniata, I received my degree with a major in sociology.

For some reason my college experience caused me to lose my taste for cornmeal mush, and there was only one thing to do with M&M's. Although my dimming eyesight required a semester out of school to learn braille and to use a tape recorder, the birds still sang outside my window. The fall air still blew my hair and lifted my spirits like a kite. The leaves still crunched under my feet. Perhaps I was even more conscious of such sensations as my vision grew worse.

I recalled a third room. It was at the Greater Pittsburgh Guild for the Blind and it did have carpet on the floor. I remember well that winter at the Guild following my graduation from college. The birds didn't sing much, and the personnel at the Guild insisted that the blinds be kept closed. But spring finally came. With a cane in my hand and a bounce in my step, I left that room and made plans to teach braille at the Hazard Vocational School, Hazard, Kentucky.

In Kentucky I found the mountains mostly comforting,

but sometimes confining; the people mostly friendly, but sometimes not understanding; the work mostly rewarding, but sometimes frustrating.

In my reminiscing at breakfast I almost forgot about the time. I flipped open my braille watch and felt the time. It was eight o'clock, and my appointment with Mr. Fletcher, director of the Rehabilitation Center, was at nine. There I would meet new people and need to cope with new experiences.

Upstairs and Down

Upstairs and Down

THE TAXI ride from the hotel to the Rehabilitation Center was as smooth as the rest of the day — well, anyway most of the day. The cab driver stopped in front of the building. He carried my bag up the flight of stairs and into the lobby. I paid him and he left. There I stood. What was I to do next?

I listened a moment. I heard typewriters somewhere to my left. Making sure my luggage was out of the way, I moved slowly toward them.

After I had taken only a few steps, my cane hit an obstruction which I assumed was a waist-high partition. I paused a moment. But before I had a chance to wonder what to do next, the typing stopped and a friendly voice from the direction of the fuzzy light asked, "May I help you?"

A smile spread across my face. The girl probably thought I was just being friendly, but that music of achievement was bubbling up inside me again.

"Yes, as a matter of fact, you may," I responded. "I'm Debby Zook and I'm looking for Mr. Fletcher."

In a moment I heard bounding footsteps on the stairs somewhere to the right of the door through which I had come. I turned expectantly.

"Miss Zook? Good to see you."

"Yes?" I responded, uncertain of myself.

"Glad you're here. I've been expecting you," said Mr. Fletcher.

"Oh, really? Well, great! I'm glad to be here and to meet you, too. I've heard a lot about this place."

"Oh, I hope it was good. How was your trip?"

"Everything worked out fine," I replied.

"Did you say you were from Hazard?" Mr. Fletcher asked.

"Yes, that's right. Way up in them thar hills," I replied and laughed.

He joined me and then added, "Well, let's go up to my office. Elevator or stairs?"

"It doesn't really matter."

"Well, let's take the elevator this time. How about an arm till you get to know the place."

I accepted his offer. "Should I leave my luggage here?"

"Oh, here, let me take it to my office. It would be safer there."

"I didn't realize this place would be large enough to have an elevator," I said.

"It's not that we are so large," Mr. Fletcher explained, "but not all the blind people with whom we work can get around as well as you can. The elevator is especially useful for those confined to wheelchairs."

"Oh, yes," I replied thoughtfully.

A moment later we were in his office. "There's a chair just to your right. Shall we have a cup of coffee?"

"Thanks, but I don't think so right now. Later, maybe." With my cane I found the chair and sat down.

"Fine. Now tell me, where did you get your training with that cane? Looks like someone did a fine job."

"The Greater Pittsburgh Guild for the Blind deserves the credit for that," I said.

The Rehabilitation Center in Louisville existed for the same purpose as the Pittsburgh Guild, he told me. Here blind people of any age could learn skills that would make it possible for them to live productively.

Mr. Fletcher knew about the Guild. So we compared notes. I discovered that the basic organization and offerings were similar, although the Center in Louisville had been operating for only a little over two years.

Mr. Fletcher took me on a tour of the building. First he showed me the Rehabilitation Center facilities on the second floor. Their classrooms were across the hall.

"This afternoon you may visit the classes in session, if you like," suggested Mr. Fletcher.

"Oh, I'd love to. That will be fun."

On the lower floor he showed me the Kentucky Industries for the Blind. Here blind persons were busily at work. Mr. Fletcher explained that they were paid by the hour for their services. He let me touch things he wanted me to "see."

"But what you have upstairs and the program down here seem so different," I commented.

"How so?" asked Mr. Fletcher.

"You train people up there so that they can find employment in the regular labor market along with sighted people," I said.

"Hopefully, yes," Mr. Fletcher agreed.

"Then why provide a special place for blind people to work?" I asked.

"I see what you mean," said Mr. Fletcher. "We do try to find employment for blind people in regular jobs. But we have to face the fact that some of our people cannot get work in other places. The reason likely has little to do with their ability to do the job, but with the reluctance of employers to hire blind workers. Yet these people want to work. So here they can achieve self-respect and take home a paycheck which they have earned. They are self-sufficient. And I'm sure you're aware how important that is to anyone's dignity."

"I guess you're right," I conceded. "I suppose I'm a bit too idealistic."

He laughed. "Time will take care of that."

But the problem of whether there should be special facilities for the blind came up again that afternoon when I was with one of the mobility instructors. He was teaching a lady to use a cane.

We went to the back of the building and up specially constructed stairs. Actually it was a long sloping hill with groups of three or four steps interspersed between long stretches of sidewalk. That was all fine, but what I could not understand was the slight drop just before the top step of each of these groups. It was constructed so that when coming from the top down, one would first feel the little dip with his feet. Then he would know the steps were right in front of him.

"Don't you teach them to use their canes to locate steps?" I asked.

"Of course," the instructor responded. "These steps are bad for teaching that skill because the blind person comes to depend on the slight dip. Steps aren't normally like these. At least I wouldn't depend on it when walking in a public place."

"Then why are they made like this?" But even as I asked I thought I knew the reason.

"Admit it, Debby, some blind people need the extra cue. Age is a big factor. Most blind people are older than you. Perhaps 40 percent of blind people are over 65. They really need this kind of thing, because the older a person is when he has to learn to find his way with a cane, the harder it is."

"Yes, I guess so. Would you say that most of the blindness after 65 is due to old age?" I asked.

"Well, I think it's rather that the major causes of blindness, cataracts and glaucoma, are more likely to occur in older people. A third major cause, diabetic retinopathy, occurs in both young and old," said the instructor.

We walked in silence for a while, his student going ahead.

"You aren't totally blind, are you?" he suddenly asked me.

"No, I can see some. Of course not enough to depend on. I can see lights and big color contrasts."

I could hear traffic. As we approached the corner, he

said, "Let's wait a minute. Here comes someone I want you to meet. He's a mobility instructor at the Kentucky School for the Blind. I guess you knew they're just down the street from us."

"Yes, I knew they were somewhere near here," I replied.

"Well, he's blind and he's teaching those kids how to use a cane."

"Oh, really. That's one thing I always thought a sighted person would need to do. I don't think I'd want a blind person to teach me how to walk. Is it safe?" I asked.

"Oh, he's legally blind, but he can still see some."

"You mean his vision is something like 20/200?"

"Yes, that's right. It works out pretty well. He stays a bit closer to his students than a sighted teacher would. He needs to be 20 feet from an object to see it like a normally sighted person would at 200 feet," he explained.

"Some legally blind people aren't really all that blind then, are they?"

He chuckled. "No, not really. Actually, only about 10 percent of the blind are totally without any sight at all."

Back in Mr. Fletcher's office I sank into the chair. It had been a big day.

"Well, what do you think? Are we as good as the Guild?" asked Mr. Fletcher.

"Of course not." I laughed good-naturedly. "Really, though, it looks like you're off to a good start."

"I'm sure there's room for improvement," he admitted.

"Thanks for showing me around. I've had a great day."

"Oh, you're welcome." Mr. Fletcher rose and walked around his desk toward me. "Jim said he'd take you to meet your bus."

"Great! Thanks."

I wasn't sure, but I thought he might be extending his hand to shake mine. I took a chance and extended mine. I was right. My hearty handshake and broad grin came from way down inside. The song was welling up inside me again.

If I Could Have Laughed

If I Could Have Laughed

"WELL, IT WAS good meeting you," Jim said as we walked toward the waiting bus for my return to Hazard. "Be sure to stop again when you're in town."

He followed me up the steps of the bus, carrying my bag.

"I sure will. And thanks for everything. I guess I'll sit right here."

"Fine. I'm putting your bag right above your head on this rack. Okay?" he said.

I agreed. Stepping sidewise into the seat, I bumped my head against the rack. We both laughed.

"I always forget about the rack being so low," I remarked.

"I bet you won't next time," he said.

"I hope you're right. Hey, thanks again."

"Well, have a good trip. See you."

I chuckled to myself as I settled into my seat. My head throbbed. He was definitely right about me remembering the next time. I took off my coat and laid it and my purse beside me.

As I put my seat in a reclining position, I decided this trip would be for thinking. I still smiled a little at the head-bumping incident.

"Thanks, God. Thanks that I can laugh about it."

I remembered the days when that wouldn't have been possible, when I was determined to keep my eye problem a well-guarded secret. For some reason I had the idea that going blind was something to be ashamed of, something really negative that I should have been able to avoid.

The eye infection responsible for my condition had started when I was eight and in the third grade. During that school year it completely destroyed the sight in one eye, and by the time it was discovered, had begun to affect the other eye. Doctors were able to slow its progress but could not stop further deterioration. My vision was nearly normal through the rest of grade school and even into junior high. Then I had to depend increasingly on glasses to continue my schooling. Soon glasses didn't even do the job. At that point, guarding the secret became a full-time obsession with me.

"What a hell I created for myself," I thought.

As a freshman in college, I pretended not to know the answers to the questions in the German text when the real problem was I couldn't see the words. And why did the professors have to write so much on the blackboard? No doubt they would have been willing to go over the work with me, but I had no intention of staying after class. That would mean letting the professor in on my secret.

I still had my driver's license then. I could get along all right yet driving by daylight, but after dark I could hardly manage. One day I drove the family car to the campus for an afternoon event. Since it was daylight when I left, all went well. I had every intention of returning home before dark. But time passed more rapidly than I realized and dusk was slipping into darkness when I started the twelve-mile trip home.

The stretch on the main highway went pretty well. I was able to follow the white lines. When I turned into Mt. Union, I nearly hit an approaching car head on. I was frightened. At the first chance, I stopped. There was no way I could drive through town. One of the hardest things I ever did was to call home from twelve blocks away and admit that I couldn't see well enough to drive the rest of the way.

The summer after my freshman year, I was hospitalized. Another doctor attempted to find the cause of my visual difficulty. Ten days later he released me. The doctor was not able to help me, and my vision grew even worse. I shuddered to realize that I was changing from "the girl with bad eyes" to "the blind girl." Now when I sat on the back steps, I couldn't tell whether or not the neighbors were in their yard. At night the moon was fuzzy and the stars had disappeared. So had my chance for continuing my college education — at least for that term.

"Man, did I hate the thought of having to learn braille," I remembered.

But my home teacher, Mr. Perry from the State Department of Rehabilitation, made regular trips to tutor me, and I learned it. There wasn't much else to do those days.

A walk around the block helped clear my mind every morning. But there were lots of things I didn't understand. Why was this happening to me?

One thing had become clear. When I went back to school that winter, I knew that my secret could no longer be kept. I had swallowed hard and prepared myself for the worst.

I PUT MY seat in an upright position. "This must be Lexington," I thought. I could tell the bus had entered a town and, according to my watch, we should be there. That meant a bus change. Gathering my things together, I waited.

When most everyone else was off, I made my way carefully down the aisle.

"Where you going, Miss?" a male voice asked. Must be the bus driver.

"Hazard."

"That's lane two. Here, can I help you?" he offered.

"Yes, thanks a lot."

"Oh, that's okay. Here you are. It should be leaving in a few minutes."

He was right. As the bus wove its way out of town, I settled back for the second half of my journey.

I RETURNED to my thinking. If I had known that the problems of adjusting to blindness were easier to solve than those created by attempting to hide my visual loss,

I would have revealed my secret much sooner. Back on campus, things went much better as I admitted my handicap. I really didn't care now who knew that I used a tape recorder and braille for taking class notes. Nor that most of my texts came on tape and what was not available on tapes, friends read to me.

Folks remarked how well I had adjusted. But I was still denying my blindness. When I stumbled over a curb, I'd tell myself it was a stupid thing to do. I was determined not to allow my handicap to keep me from living life to the full. I wanted to experience all those things I would have enjoyed with normal eyesight.

I lived for the moments when I became so involved in something, anything, that I would forget for a while that I was blind. But I was reminded of my limitations at every turn — when professors wrote on the blackboard or handed out mimeographed class outlines, when I needed to buy something at the bookstore, or even when I had to find a place to sit in the cafeteria.

The tires of the bus hummed on the pavement beneath me. I smiled to myself as I remembered the time I lost my tray in the school cafeteria. It wasn't funny then. I usually ate with friends, but that day I was alone. The school cafeteria was arranged in such a way that it was more convenient to set down one's tray on a table before picking up a beverage. I usually paid close attention to the number of rows of tables I was from a fixed point, but that day I failed to do so. When I was ready to return to my table with my drink, I suddenly had no idea where I had put my tray. I knew it was at a round table but many of them were round.

After a few minutes of walking around tables and gliding my fingers over the tops of them, carrying a glass of milk in the other hand, and trying not to look conspicuous, I came to a dead stop. I'd have died if I had thought someone was watching me. My psychology prof came along just then and quietly helped me get my bearings again.

"If I could have laughed then, God, it would have been a lot easier on me," I confessed.

Since I had been out of school for a term, I graduated one term behind my class. The day after my last final exam, I left for the Greater Pittsburgh Guild for the Blind. My vision had been getting steadily worse and I finally had been talked into going for special training. But I hated the thought of learning to walk with a cane just as much as I despised needing to study braille three years before.

I swallowed hard as I walked into the front doors of the Guild's main building. If I had known that the Guild would teach me to laugh at myself and my problems, I'd have been less apprehensive.

"Thanks a lot for helping me, God," I prayed as the bus sped on.

Those were tough days. Finally I had to look myself right in the eye and say emphatically, but tearfully, "I am blind."

"I know you don't want your handicap to affect your life," Mr. Wood, my counselor, had said. "But it's going to anyway. You can work around it and adjust to it, but you have to admit that it's there."

I hurried back to my room, shut the door, and threw my cane down as hard as I could. Then I buried my head in my pillow and cried. Unconditionally accepting my blindness seemed to build a limiting wall around my life.

But I soon discovered this was not the case at all. Honestly admitting my blindness was actually setting me free.

The step-by-step adjustment had been a long, difficult process. All the way from guarding my secret from the world, to just keeping the secret from myself, to letting even myself in on it. I had wondered what the next step would be. Perhaps I could laugh my way into it, I had decided.

I braced myself on the arm of the seat as the bus went around a sharp turn. We must be close to Hazard. I checked my watch. Ten minutes yet, if the bus was on time.

A Few Weeks of Humility

A Few Weeks of Humility

IT WAS toward evening when the bus pulled into the station at Hazard. I hoped I could get a cab. Usually, I had no trouble.

When I first came to Hazard, I was determined to remain as independent as possible. I had expected some form of public transportation, but there was none. At first I was uncertain whether or not I should pay for cab fare just to have a little independence.

A moment's deliberation gave me the answer. It might seem a lot to pay, but for now it was worth it. Soon I'd have friends who would come to the bus station and meet me because they were my friends, not because I was blind and they pitied me.

So as I stepped off the bus and walked toward the front street, I replied in the affirmative to a driver who asked, "Would you like a cab?"

Soon I was on my way home.

As the cab pulled up alongside my apartment building, I opened my purse to pay him. "Oh, I don't have any dollar bills. How about a five?" I asked.

I held out the five to him while he rummaged in his pockets for some change.

"Do you mind if I ask you a question, Miss?"

"Probably not," I answered. "Depends on what you ask."

"How do you know that's a five? Can you tell by the feel of it? I've heard tell of blind folk who can."

I smiled again but looked away. Usually, I was glad when people felt free enough to ask me that.

Sometimes I would just tell them that I couldn't tell bills apart by their feel and that I had to depend on the honesty of others. The inquirer would always reassure me that no one in these parts would ever cheat someone like me. The implication, of course, was that anyone who would treat a poor blind girl that way was a real scoundrel.

Sometimes I would tell them in detail how I folded my fives in halves, my tens in fourths, and kept my twenties in another part of my billfold. That helped remove the idea that blind or other handicapped people possess some kind of superhuman abilities. I mean, anyone can fold money.

But this time I replied, "I've heard of people like that, too. I haven't figured out how they do it. No, I can't tell by the feel. Maybe I've never had enough money to learn that skill." We both chuckled.

"Thanks a lot," I replied as I accepted my change,

put it away, and reached for the car door handle.

"Wait, I'll help you up those steps. You might fall."

"No, thanks. I can make it."

I jumped out, got my bag, and started up the steps. They weren't the best steps in the world and there was no railing. But this was not the first time I had walked up them. Sure I might fall, but I'd take the chance. I had dreaded the thought of using a cane, but this kind of independence was precisely why I used it. I wanted to be able to walk up steps, or anywhere, alone and with confidence.

Inside the apartment, I flipped on a light, took off my coat, pushed a tape into my stereo, and flopped down on the couch. My roommate, a nurse who worked nights, wouldn't be home for a while yet.

Yes, I had much for which to thank the Greater Pittsburgh Guild for the Blind. Not just my cane travel. The weeks I spent there were good weeks. Well, extremely helpful, if not always good.

Before I went, as part of my rebellion, I had announced, "I'm going there to learn. If they can't teach me anything I don't already know, I'm not staying. If there are ever three consecutive days there when I haven't learned anything new, I'm leaving."

But I never left. I never even thought of leaving.

I was one of approximately thirty trainees of various ages and degrees of blindness, and from many walks of life. Attitudes toward blindness varied from simply denying it to using it for personal exploitation.

Individualized schedules were typical of the personalized attention provided by the Guild. Classes, such as visualization, where the vision of one's mind is sharpened, and communication, which emphasizes social skills, might include up to five or six trainees. But others, like sensory training, where one learns that his other senses are just as reliable as his sight once was, usually operate on a one-to-one basis.

I found some of the classes a bit humiliating. It was not so much the class, I guess, as my pride. The class called techniques of daily living (T.D.L.) emphasizes the really practical aspects of everyday life. We practiced using braille watches; taking care of our hair, nails, and skin; shaving; polishing shoes; and using games modified for the blind. Such things I could handle.

But when the class marched to the dining room to practice eating, especially cutting meat, I had to have a little talk with myself. It wasn't that I couldn't use a few tips here and there and a lot of practice. But how humiliating! There I was, a college graduate, learning to cut meat.

But I managed to stay with it. I convinced myself that a few weeks of humility might lead to a lifetime of dignity. Counseling sessions were especially helpful in instilling within me new confidence that I could cope with my blindness — although this didn't come without considerable inner struggles.

Another class was kinesiatrics. The mats, exercise bicycle, rowing machine, treadmill, balance beam, and punching bag made it obvious what this class was for.

On one occasion, I had hoped to slip in late unnoticed. But the instructor saw me come in and came over to me. Quietly he asked, "Have you just come from counseling?"

I could only nod. That was all he expected. I guessed

he smiled. I felt him squeeze my shoulder as he handed me the boxing gloves for the punching bag and said, "Go to it."

Learning to sew, cook, iron, and clean provided needed skills and additional confidence. There were other classes, too. For many, braille and mobility were the most valuable. I already knew braille pretty well, so a bit of brushing up was all I needed.

But mobility was a different story. Thinking back now, I feel sorry for my instructor. Miss Joy Mallard was remarkably patient with me. More than once when she was explaining a certain way one should handle the cane for a given situation, I had remarked, "Now that's the stupidest thing I've heard yet. What's the point of that?"

There always was a point, of course, and Miss Mallard would explain it thoroughly. Then she'd add, "You have a right to think it's stupid, but you also owe it to yourself to use it well before completely making up your mind."

When I started walking with a cane, she repeatedly told me to slow down.

"Before I had a cane, I had to walk slowly because I was uncertain what was ahead," I argued. "That's one reason I wanted to learn to use the cane — so I don't have to poke along."

Somehow Miss Mallard got through to me that it was not a matter of speed but of poise, grace, and just generally looking good.

Looking good? With a cane? Well, if that was possible I would try it. But the idea that cane travel was an art certainly was a new one.

"Hold your head up and be proud you're a woman," she advised.

"You mean it's still possible to do that?" I asked.

"Why not?" Miss Mallard replied.

She made it seem reasonable, so I had tried. It was a whole new attitude I was building, and I thought I was going to like it.

Sometimes she would stop right in the middle of a lesson and ask if I had read a certain book. I read a lot using the talking book machine. It played recordings of books read by professionals. She always asked me about my reading at the moment I was becoming intensely frustrated with my walking lesson. She knew it would relieve the tension for both of us.

I didn't know then that mastering the skills of cane travel and independent living would not be the end of the problems related to my blindness. The problems would merely change from those of learning independent living to *convincing others* that I could do so. If I had known this at the time, perhaps I would not have been so eager to learn.

People always meant well. But I soon discovered that this didn't always help.

Well-Meaning Friends

Well-Meaning Friends

I WAS certain the old man I met on the streets of downtown Pittsburgh during my training by the Guild meant well. The Guild itself was located outside the Pittsburgh city limits, but my instructor, Miss Mallard, often took me to the Golden Triangle for mobility lessons in crossing streets. On this particular day, Miss Mallard had directed me to make my own way through pedestrians and traffic and to meet her several blocks down the street.

As I was walking along, intent on using my cane correctly, I was joined by an elderly man. From the tremor in his voice and the odor that reached me, I concluded that he had just stepped from a bar. He walked alongside me for a while before he asked, "Are you really blind?"

51

I had never been asked the question before in that way, and it took me off guard. When I admitted what he already suspected, he said that it was a great pity. I chuckled to myself as I thought how right he was.

That was not the end though. This obviously lonely man began telling me the story of his life, how he had been all over the world. I could catch only half of what he was saying. I walked as fast as I dared, only talking when I had to, but he kept right beside me.

Soon we came to a street corner. Miss Mallard had instructed me not to accept help during this lesson. I was to listen to the traffic. Since I was on the right side of the street, my cue was to be the idling motor of the car behind me to my left. The car would be waiting for the light to turn green. I was to start across the street immediately when the light changed. I would know when that happened by listening to his motor. The second I heard the motor accelerating, I was to step off the curb and start across the street. If he turned right, I would be in the middle of the intersection by the time he got there. He could easily see me since he would probably have been watching me on the curb as he waited for the light.

I tried to block out the chatter of the man beside me and review this procedure as I approached the corner. I waited for several cycles of cues to get my timing right, hoping my "friend" would go on.

But the old gentleman had other ideas. "Here, girlie, I'll help you across." He grabbed my arm.

I stood firm. "Keep control of every situation," my instructor had drilled me. "Don't let anyone shove you around, literally."

I explained to the man as clearly as I could, "I'm on a mobility lesson with the Guild for the Blind and want to do this myself."

Finally he gave up and crossed the street alone.

At least I thought he had given up. But I was wrong. A few seconds later, he called from the middle of the intersection, "Come on, baby. You can come across now!"

From the sound of the horns that started blowing, I knew he was probably holding out his arms, bringing traffic to a dead stop.

"Well, I guess I don't have to cross that street," I thought as I turned and started down another direction. For some reason, I could not bring myself to trust that man's judgment. But he had a mind of his own, and started after me, muttering as he came. Then I really began getting scared.

What was I to do? How relieved I was to hear a friendly voice by my side saying, "Grab on." It was my instructor. I took her arm and we quickly headed another direction. She had observed the whole episode.

Mobility lessons were not the only occasions when well-meaning friends caused problems. Another incident happened in Frankfort, Kentucky, in front of the state office building. I was attending a statewide conference on vocational education for the blind. One of the group was Paul Collins, placement specialist with the Division for the Blind for the state of Kentucky.

I had worked with Paul on other projects such as radio and television shows in Hazard. Though he was legally blind, his visual acuity was much better than mine. Often when I was with him I did not use my cane and depended on him. This usually worked out quite well.

It was about five minutes till starting time. The group, which included two others besides Paul and me, was walking casually up the front sidewalks toward the building. The two sets of steps proved to be no problem. Not until we got to the front door did Paul remember that he had left his briefcase in the car, parked half a block away.

"Come on, D. J.," he called as he wheeled around and took off in the other direction to get it. I knew D. J. meant me — Deborah Jane. I thought perhaps he should go himself, but I took off with him anyway.

At the first set of steps, he paused momentarily. I picked up the cue and ran down the steps with him. He forgot to give me the cue at the second set. As he hurried down them, I went flying through the air in a most undignified way. I landed on my feet, fortunately, with his arm firmly in my grip. I started to tell him what I thought of his carelessness.

"Tell me later," he protested. "We've got to run now." He wouldn't have been able to hear me anyway. He was laughing too hard. But it was quite a while before I was able to laugh at that one.

On another occasion, Paul Collins and I were interviewing a few potential students in a town south of Lexington. The meeting was over, and the three — Paul, myself, and his secretary, who did the driving and bookwork — were heading for the car. Paul knew that I could see sharp contrasts such as the difference between the white sidewalk and the dark blacktop of the parking lot we were approaching. He also knew that I determined when to step up or down by his body movements, which was quite easy with my hand on his arm. This time there was no step. The sidewalk and the parking lot were on the same level.

But when he came to the end of the sidewalk and was stepping into the parking lot, he bent his knees enough to make me think there was a step. I fell right into his trap and took an awkward step down. He thought it was a big joke. An instant later, when I had recovered my balance, I joined him in laughter.

Although blindness sometimes is the cause of a humorous incident, at other times it's a more serious threat to people's safety. During a month's vacation at home from my work in Hazard, my mother took me to see a doctor in downtown Philadelphia. His office was in a big building with at least four elevators and lots of people milling about. I liked to be as independent as possible. Even though my mother was with me, I was using my cane.

Since we were the last ones on the elevator going down, we were the first ones to get off. When the door opened, I extended my cane to make sure the way was clear before stepping out. I did not realize a lady was walking past the front of the elevator door. The cane caught her right between the ankles as she was taking a step. She stumbled and, to my horror, fell flat on the floor in front of me.

My mother helped her to her feet and made sure she was all right. I apologized. I wished the people observing the incident would have rebuked me soundly. But neither the lady nor any of the bystanders reprimanded me.

I had done only what I had been instructed to do. But I was aware of a new hazard and resolved to be more careful in similar situations in the future. I mulled over the incident as I went down the street with my mother.

An Hour of Heaven

An Hour of Heaven

IN MY CONVERSATIONS with other people who cannot see, I've heard many unfortunate accounts of experiences they had as children, often involving their own families.

Sometimes parents are so ashamed of a blind child they won't take him out in public. They refuse to let him learn to know other persons. Often they won't let him do anything for himself. Parents may not want their blind child to become educated, nor be willing to help seek out a suitable job for him. They may not be able to help him understand that he, too, is a person of as much worth as anyone who sees.

I admit that blindness is a handicap. But because a person is blind does not say he is also deaf, speechless, and unable to think and learn, or that he cannot do things for himself or function as a person in his own right.

Sighted people also have handicaps. They may have heart trouble, one leg or arm, cancer, deafness, or some other ailment. This is not considered as a personal disgrace. Then why should a blind person be ashamed of his handicap? Why should parents be ashamed of a blind child who so desperately needs their love and care? Why should they deprive him of his rights to be a whole person as God intends?

I'm happy to tell you my case was different. My eye problem began with the annual eye examination in the third grade. My school nurse sent a note to my parents that I was blind in one eye. Then things began to happen. Throughout all the difficult experiences accompanying this handicap my parents, and especially my mother after father's death, did their best to help me.

A few days after the blindness was discovered, I found myself confined to the Will's Eye Hospital in Philadelphia. Only eight, I felt too young to be left alone two hundred miles from home. My mother and father thought so, too. But he had church responsibilities and she had four other young children.

My life centered around the one hour every other day when my parents made that long trip to visit me. The children's ward was on the third floor, and we patients were forbidden to go out in the hall. So at ten till seven every other evening, I would take up my post in the doorway. From there I could see down the hall to the elevator.

Those were the longest ten-minute periods of my life. Finally seven o'clock would roll around, the elevator door would open, and a stream of parents would come flowing out into the hall. I could never understand how so many people could get into one elevator.

Nor could I understand how my parents were the first ones out, but they usually were. Then, forgetting all nurses' warnings, I would dash down the hall and my hour of heaven would begin.

I never tired of this little scene. I'm sure my parents must have, since they returned home again after each visit, traveling the 200 miles to face another day of responsibilities.

Only once did this pattern change. All had proceeded as usual up to the time when the elevator door opened. As I was ready to do my sprint down the hall, I realized that my parents were not the first ones coming out. More than that, they were not the second or third ones. Although the elevator held just as many as it always had, it was not enough. Other parents were coming down the hall. They hurried past me to see their children. The elevator doors went shut, and I was still standing there too stunned even to cry.

I was too young to realize that these trips cost money and that my older sister, Brenda, was staying home from school to take care of my little brother and sister who were still preschoolers. It didn't occur to me that our not-so-new family car would soon be complaining about all this extra running. All I knew was that the elevator had come and gone and I was still standing there alone.

I was about to cry when the elevator door opened again with another load of parents. I was almost afraid to look for fear they would not be among these either.

61

But they were! I couldn't help crying as I ran down the hall toward them. They had been two minutes late and had missed the first load.

I still don't understand why it was only two minutes. Their car had broken down on the Pennsylvania Turnpike. Knowing they had a limited time to get to the hospital, they hailed a Greyhound bus and it brought them into Philadelphia. To this day I don't know how they got back to the car that night, managed to get it repaired, and returned home.

Even when I was old enough to understand the disruption my eye problems brought into my parents' lives, they never complained.

They tried hard not to give me special treatment. My father worked part time as custodian at the nearby grade school where I attended. We kids found it interesting to go with him, emptying the trash cans and helping him move the desks while he swept. Although I had one eye removed during my seven-week stay in Philadelphia, I had twenty-twenty vision in the remaining eye. The experiments and treatments I had been given left me feeling weak, but I still wanted to help.

I watched my father many times and helped him often. I asked him if I could do a room by myself.

"That's a lot of work for one person to do alone," he reminded me. "You have to move all those desks, sweep, and then move all the desks back in place."

"Yes, I know, but let me do just one room," I begged. "I'll do it good."

"Well, okay. But when you get tired, just quit and I'll finish."

Certain I wouldn't get tired, I set about eagerly

cleaning the room just the way my father would have done it. When I was about half through, he completed what he was doing in the building and went home. He told me to come when I was finished. But that second half of the room seemed much larger than the first half. My determination was all that kept me going.

It was starting to get dark outside, and I was beginning to have a great deal more respect for my father who usually cleaned ten or twelve of these huge rooms in one night. It became harder and harder to see the piles of dirt that I had swept to the end of the row. I was afraid I'd have to stop because I could no longer see where I had swept and where I hadn't.

By the time I heard his footsteps coming down the hall, I was at a total loss to know how he could do janitor work at night as he often did. As he stepped into the room, he reached over and flipped the light switch.

"Why don't you turn on the lights, Debby?" he asked. "When I didn't see a light over here, I thought you'd left."

No one in the world could have felt more foolish. I had forgotten to turn on the lights! I looked around at the floor and saw the little piles of dirt I had missed here and there because of the darkness. It had come so gradually, and I had been so intent on my work that the need to turn on a light hadn't even occurred to me.

Not long after this, we moved from the parsonage to a house about four blocks away. There, too, I did my share of the work and received no special protection even though I was as daring as most kids. Like the time I bet my older brother, Fred, that he could not tie me up so securely I could not get untangled. He chuckled, accepted my challenge, tied me up tightly, and left me alone. Only after I yelled loudly enough to make myself heard above the house noises, did someone come to my rescue. My family found my physical defect no reason for pity.

Two years later our family moved to Ohio so my father could find work. There I became more conscious of the deep concern my parents had regarding my vision. My mother and I went to visit the sixth-grade teacher at my new school.

"I think she should know about your eyes, Debby," my mother replied to my protests. "That way there won't be any misunderstandings."

Then my father died from a cancerous brain tumor and we moved back to Pennsylvania. All through high school, as my vision gradually worsened, my mother had to face decisions alone relating to my handicap. At one point she arranged for home instruction for me. I'm sure she sensed that I was growing more and more sensitive about being different from other kids. No doubt she was torn between keeping me happy by playing my game with me and knowing that I would not really be happy until I accepted my difference.

When I went off to college, she did all in her power to help me. She was limited, though, because there were things I would not allow her to do for me. Even though I may have been wrong, she respected my wishes.

"Debby, it would be a whole lot better if your teachers knew you were having trouble seeing. They could explain what they put on the board and give you extra help."

"I don't want extra help," I protested. "Why should

64

they give me any more help than they give the other students?" And if I was aware of why I needed extra help, I wouldn't admit it even to myself.

Finally, after the semester I stayed out of school to learn braille, I agreed that perhaps the professors should know. My mother went along and we visited each teacher I would have the next term. We explained my situation and made whatever arrangements were necessary. Mother stayed with me all the way.

When the time came for me to begin my job at Hazard, Kentucky, Mother offered to take me down. She would help me find a place to live and assist me in getting oriented to my new environment. Although it must have been hard, she consented when I said I wanted to go myself. Now, as I look back on that first week, I think I understand a little of why she was anxious for me.

Flowers at the Desk

Flowers at the Desk

"CALL US as soon as you get there and settled, will you?" my uncle, Ellrose Zook, requested as I got my things together to board the plane for Lexington at the Pittsburgh Airport. I was headed for Hazard, Kentucky, and my new job. I had said good-bye to my reluctant mother a few hours before at the Somerset interchange of the Pennsylvania Turnpike, where she and I had met my uncle and aunt. Ellrose and Frances had brought me the rest of the way.

"All right, I will," I reassured him. "I'll be okay."

The airline's passenger-service man was waiting. I took his arm and we boarded the plane. I couldn't figure out why Ellrose and Frances and my mother were so concerned. True, I hadn't met my employer yet and didn't have a place to live, but that didn't seem sufficient grounds for so much worrying. I wasn't really so sure that everything would work out smoothly, but after all, half of the fun and excitement of experiencing new things was the element of uncertainty. I guess that's why I was looking forward to this trip. I was anxious to discover how God would work things out for me. I was sure that He would, and I was soon to discover anew His wonderful care for me.

As the plane took off, I thought of my mother. I guess she was used to me getting excited about uncertainty and being thrilled by risky things. I wondered if she still remembered the time I got lost as a preschool child in the five and ten store in Mount Union. She was nowhere to be found, so I assumed she had gone home. Although I didn't understand why she would leave town without me, I figured it was my responsibility to get home by myself. And when neighbors saw a five-year-old girl who "looked for all the world like Leroy Zook's girl," trudging along the highway leading to where I lived, they offered me a ride. Naturally, I accepted. My mother hadn't deserted me, of course. At that moment she was contacting the Mount Union police, reporting a missing child. As a last resort she called home, and there I was, wondering what was taking her so long.

I decided that my love of the unknown and need for independence must be related in some way to my love for the Indians. I always enjoyed stories about the Indians of early America from the Indians' point of view. If I'd had my choice about where and when to be born, I'd have chosen to come as an Indian boy in the days before the white man arrived to harass them. Perhaps this desire was based more on fictitious stories than facts; however, the reason remained the same. I liked the freedom that I associated with their way of life, the independence and the thrill of the unknown.

My limited eyesight in college complicated somewhat my tendency to seek out uncertain situations. I wondered how my mother felt about the trip I made to Fort Lauderdale, Florida, with some other students from the area. We were all members of Inter-Varsity Christian Fellowship, an interdenominational organization for college students. Along with several hundred other college students, we were planning to meet on the Florida beach that Easter vacation during my sophomore year. We wanted to share our Christian faith with the thousands of other college students who would be gathering there for a week of fun in the sun.

My vision was not good enough for me to be completely independent. I would need help from time to time. But Mother did not protest when I suggested the idea to her. No one else from Juniata College was planning to go, and I didn't know the other students who were helping to pay for the car which the Inter-Varsity staff worker decided to rent to take us from Pennsylvania to Florida.

We traveled straight through, well over twenty hours. By the time we arrived in front of the Holiday Inn on the beach, we knew each other pretty well. Then I experienced one of the little miracles that made this kind of trip exciting. I was reassured again that God was with me. We had made our reservations through Inter-Varsity, and they in turn had assigned us to rooms in groups of three or four. We had no choice of roommates. I was quite surprised to discover that,

71

of the several hundred possibilities, one of the girls I had ridden with from Pennsylvania was to share my room. I took this as confirmation from God that the week would be a profitable one. And it was.

Then there was the time I decided to go to Urbana, Illinois, where Inter-Varsity was holding its triennial missionary conference. I was a senior and this was my last chance to go as a student.

Several others from my college were joining a bus-load going from central Pennsylvania. Over ten thousand students were expected to attend. We were to have our meetings at the University of Illinois and live on campus. Here, too, room assignments had been made prior to our arrival. This time I discovered I was alone. None of the students from Pennsylvania was even assigned to the same building where I was to stay. Was I discouraged? No, I decided I would like it. It would be another adventure for me full of opportunities.

That was a good week, also. Scary moments were balanced against moments of reassurance. One morning I was to meet a new friend at the northwest entrance of the huge hall in which the convention was meeting. He called me the night before, having noticed my name on a roster. His name was Zook, too. He thought I might know the whereabouts of an old friend of his who was also a Zook. I had never heard of her but we talked for a long time anyway. We decided it would be fun to have lunch together the following day. He agreed to meet me at this entrance. Since we had not seen each other before, recognizing each other among so many persons coming and going could be hard.

"I'll have some flowers at the desk for you in the morning," he told me. "Wear them so I'll know which one is you." I didn't mention that I could not see well, for fear he would drop me as a dinner date. It was a perfect plan but it didn't work because there were no flowers at the desk the next morning. I was a few minutes late arriving at the northwest entrance but was sure all would be fine. I waited. And waited. I didn't have the flowers on and I couldn't have seen him standing around, but I waited anyway. Lots of people came and went. Thirty minutes later, things had begun to settle down and I was still waiting. I knew I could not get back to the dorm alone. One needed to go by bus and this was before my cane days. I was pretty dependent on others.

"God, please let me know what I should do," I prayed. "And by the way, what's the point of misunderstanding?" And I waited some more.

"Hey, Debby, fancy meeting you here!" Familiar voices approached me. "How are you doing?"

"Fine," I said, extending my hand. They were friends from Pennsylvania whom I had not seen in several months.

"What are you doing? Waiting to meet someone?"

"As a matter of fact, I am," I replied.

I explained my situation. My friends looked around and, finding no one who appeared to be looking for me, they suggested I come with them. They were on their way to lunch and would help me board the right bus back to my dorm after we ate together. Of all the kids who passed me while I was waiting, why had these old friends happened to come by just at the time I needed someone? I knew it was more than a coincidence. God was watching over me. Once again I realized I was in good hands and could relax.

The misunderstanding with the Zook fellow eventually was resolved. The flowers had arrived late. When he couldn't find me, he hadn't lingered long. When I got back to my dorm late that afternoon, I learned that he had been trying to reach me by phone. We finally did get together and had an enjoyable evening meal. So, as things worked out, I had the dinner date plus the bonus of a meal with old friends. God had things under control the whole time.

The plane was landing now at Lexington. I brought my thoughts back to the present. I hoped my Kentucky friends would be there to meet me. I was sure God had this situation well under control, too. Knowing this freed me from the fear which usually accompanies new and unknown situations.

I didn't realize then how my simple confidence in God would be shaken by the events of the coming week.

A Hook on the Wall

A Hook on the Wall

DOUG AND Willa Grant were waiting inside the door at the Lexington Airport. Things were going to be fine, I just knew it.

"Long time, no see." I recognized Doug's voice immediately.

"Hi, Doug. Hi, Willa. Boy, it's sure nice of you both to come and get me."

"Oh, don't mention it. We're glad to. Let's check for your luggage. How many pieces did you have?"

"Just three. Here are the stubs for them. The luggage is blue." And Doug was off.

"Say, where did you get that stick?" Willa asked. "You didn't have it last summer, did you?"

No, I hadn't had a cane the previous summer when I had been in Kentucky as a part of the Summer Appalachian Seminar, a program directed by Mennonite Central Committee (MCC) in cooperation with Eastern Mennonite College and various service agencies of eastern Kentucky. I had been assigned to teach a summer braille class at Hyden working with the Office of Economic Opportunity.

Doug and Willa were also working in Kentucky under MCC. Doug was serving a term of Voluntary Service in place of military duty because of his beliefs about war. Doug and Willa had made my summer easier. Doug had recruited braille students before the summer began, and he assisted me after I arrived in ordering supplies and working out transportation problems for the students who were taking the class.

I was genuinely grateful for all their past help and especially now that they had come to Lexington to meet me.

The drive to Hazard took a little over two hours. It was late Friday night when we arrived at the Grant residence, a large country house with a fireplace as the only source of heat. But the hospitality was superb, and there was plenty of sleeping space. A door set on several concrete blocks with a foam rubber mattress laid on top made a reasonably comfortable bed.

The next day we tried to find a place for me to rent, an apartment, or even a room. But nothing suitable seemed to be available. Monday I was to report for work.

"I think I'll call the Vocational School first thing," I commented to Willa over hot tea at breakfast Monday morning.

"Do you have to be there by a certain time?"

"No, nothing was ever said about the time. It's all beginning to seem a bit vague. Mr. Prater told me my first class would be today. And as far as I know, I'm to have only one student."

The telephone call told me nothing more than I was to come to the school. As far as the time was concerned, well, any time would be fine. I was still sure things were in good hands, all the way to the school. While waiting to see Mr. Prater, the director of the school, some doubts began to rise in my mind.

The interview went fine, though. I was reassured of my position as teacher of braille. Mr. Prater was a pleasant enough man.

He asked about my college days and about my cane and the kind of help I would need.

"I'll not need any more help in getting around than anyone else would," I insisted to his surprise. "Just give me a good tour of the building and I'll be fine," I assured him. "Of course I may need help with reading material occasionally."

"We can work that out," he agreed.

There was a pause. I became uneasy. Pauses always did that to me. I didn't know if he was looking at something on his desk, gazing out the window, or staring at me. This made it hard to know how I was expected to respond. So I just waited.

"We have only one student — a girl," he said finally, with a note of apology in his voice.

"Yes, that's what I thought you'd said," I replied.

"There may be more after you get started, but she'll be your only responsibility for now. Let me see if I can call her now. She is the one who really pushed for this class. Excuse me a minute." He lifted the phone, dialed another office, and asked the person who answered to come to his desk.

Another pause. "Mrs. Ihrig knows where to reach her," he said as a lady walked into his office. "Could you see if you can get hold of Miss Merrill for me, please. Oh, and this is Miss Zook, who's here to teach her braille."

I smiled in response to her welcome, but a moment later I felt like crying.

"Yes, I'll try," Mrs. Ihrig was saying, "but I think she's out of town. I believe she went to Ohio for her brother's funeral. But let me try." With that she left the room.

Now what? I had come alone all the way to Kentucky for my first job. Now it appeared that "my job" was in another state.

"By the way," Mr. Prater interrupted my thoughts, "do you have a place to stay?"

"I've been looking but haven't found anything yet," I responded. "It isn't easy."

He agreed that suitable housing might be hard to find. "Maybe we can help," he suggested as Mrs. Ihrig came back into his room.

"I can't get hold of Miss Merrill," she said. "I don't know when she'll be back, but I wouldn't expect her to be gone more than a week."

I tried to smile. It wasn't easy right then.

They did help me find a place. It wasn't the best room in the world, but it had a bed, a bureau, and a hook on the wall. It was better than nothing. They told me that as soon as Miss Merrill was back in town and could

80

be reached, they would call me. That seemed logical. What else was there to say?

By Wednesday, I had read through all the braille books I had brought with me. I'd read them all before, but re-reading them was better than staring into space. I also had arranged and rearranged my things in the one dresser allotted to me and hung as many of my clothes as I dared on the single hook on the wall.

Doug and Willa had taken me to get groceries, so I had plenty to eat. But the landlady was hesitant about letting me use the gas stove in her kitchen. I was limited to the hot plate she set in the room for me. But that was better than nothing.

By Thursday I vowed I'd wait a week and only a week. This whole thing was silly anyway. Why hadn't I been content to stay at home? I could have taken a job there — a job that didn't depend on the absence or presence of one person.

Why couldn't I sit back like other blind people I knew. I was drawing Social Security and the payments would continue until I proved I could support myself. I knew I could get by without working. But that was the problem. I didn't want just to get by. I wanted a good life. But even more than that, I wanted to prove that I was a capable person in my own right.

I guess I was proving it mostly to myself. Others already seemed to accept me. Putting myself in a place where I would either swim or drown seemed a tough way of making my point, especially when I was pushed under every time my head came up for air.

If I could just get out of my confining room for a break. I'd been given no orientation to the surrounding area, however. I knew the house where I lived wasn't far from the school, but I had also been told that it was too far to walk and that there was no sidewalk. But there was a road outside the front door. I should be able to walk alongside it without getting lost. If I walked for a while, then turned around and came back the same distance, all would be well.

I took my coat from the hanger and my cane from the corner of the room and headed for the door.

"Where are you going, Debby?" It was the voice of my landlady. I had planned to go without giving anyone the chance to tell me it was silly and unsafe.

"Just out for a little bit. I'll be right back and I'll be all right," I assured her.

She protested but soon found that I had made up my mind. She stood at the door and watched as I started off, unsure of myself. Now that I was outside, which way should I go? I had a foggy idea that the Vocational School was off to the left. Using my cane as carefully as I could, I came to the edge of the concrete porch and stepped down. A car went by and I knew I was on the street.

The concrete porch would be my landmark. On my way back I would know I was home by the feel of this porch. Now to stay close to the side. I was on my way.

I took a deep breath. It certainly was nice out here. And to think, I'd been cooped up in the house all that time when I could have come outside. But it had been raining most of the time anyway. Well, it was good being out now. After a while I came to an uneven place in the road and discovered it was a set of railroad tracks — probably an abandoned line, I thought. Soon the road turned. As I followed it cautiously around the bend, a truck pulled up beside me.

"You going to the Vocational School?" a young male voice inquired.

I stopped. Should I turn around and head back to the house, ignoring him, or should I accept this as an opportunity to find out how to go to the school?

"Yes," I replied cautiously. "Am I headed the right way?"

"No, you shouldn't have turned right. It's up that way." Probably he was pointing.

"Get in. We'll take you to the school," he offered. The tone of his voice didn't sound quite right to me, so I refused. I turned and walked back toward the house. The truck pulled up beside me again and another male asked, "Where do you live?" I wasn't sure what the name of the game was, but I was getting the idea that it wasn't "Good Samaritan."

"Oh, down the road here," I answered and kept walking. And I easily found the house. I had proved my independence again.

Friday came and I still had heard nothing from the school. I vowed to leave Monday if they had not called. But the weekend — why waste it?

I made a few phone calls and discovered that some friends, whom I met the summer before, would be home and would pick me up in Hyden if I got there by bus. So I packed a few things in a little bag and called a cab. I thought I was allowing plenty of time — fifteen minutes. But it wasn't enough. I missed the bus. I didn't even get out of the cab. The driver had seen the bus sitting there before, and it wasn't there now, so I just told him to take me back. I could get another bus Saturday morning. That would cut my weekend short, but it was better than nothing.

It rained all night and people kept talking about high water. I tried to ignore it. I had never lived in a place where flooding was a problem, and I was afraid that this might cut my weekend trip out all together. It had stopped raining by Saturday morning though there were still reports of flooded areas. Some of my land-lady's friends offered to take me to the bus station. I accepted and was thankful for their thoughtfulness.

A bus was waiting in front of the station. I got in, grateful finally to be on my way. Just to be on the safe side, I asked another passenger if this was the bus to Hyden. It wasn't. I should have checked before I boarded it. I got off quickly. The folks who had brought me to the station were still there. The bus to Hyden had been canceled because of high water. I asked if they could take me home. I hoped they couldn't tell I was on the verge of crying. I looked out the window and answered their questions about where I had planned to go in Hyden.

We drove a while. The conversation turned to other things. Gradually I became aware that we were going somewhere other than back to the house.

After a while the driver turned to me and announced, "This is Hyden. Which way did you say it was from here?"

What do you say when a total stranger takes you from a weekend of loneliness and sets you on the doorstep of friends?

The weekend was a good one. I returned to Hazard

84

and the call to teach came on Monday. The class started, feebly at first, and life began to settle down to a routine.

But the problems did not stop there. The proving continued. Sometimes it looked as though I would go under and never learn to swim after all. Sometimes no one was even there to see me go under. But whenever there was real danger, a total stranger, turned friend, would reach out a hand.

The day would come when I could relax and be myself. Then I would feel confident that I was a normal, useful person even though I was blind.

I had always been treated with respect by my family and friends. No one did my work for me at home or hesitated to let me know if my work wasn't up to par. Nor did my family withhold praise when I did anything worth commending. They treated me like a human being at every point along the way.

Any proving I did now was mainly for my own benefit — and perhaps for my new associates. I knew the people back home believed in me. I wasn't sure of my new friends.

Perhaps all of these inner struggles were unnecessary — but how could I do otherwise?

Too Proud to Fall

Too Proud to Fall

IT WAS TO be an important day on campus. The Vocational School was holding a public hearing. Citizens from the Hazard area and other nearby places would be on hand, as well as people from the State Department of Education at Frankfort. All was in shipshape condition, and everyone was on good behavior.

Blind people do not all feel they have to prove themselves, as I did. But I set high standards for myself and was not satisfied unless I met them. My personal goals were so high, however, that meeting them was next to impossible. I could excuse something in another person, who could see, much quicker than I could permit myself the same mistake. It all came to a head on the day of the public hearing.

I had left the cafeteria and was heading across campus

following a midmorning coffee break. I knew the layout of the buildings, curbs, and trash cans quite well by that time. As I walked along, I was not paying much attention to these details and was not using my cane as carefully as I should have.

I was unaware of some new signs that had been temporarily set up for the benefit of the visitors. As I stepped off the curb, my foot caught on the base of one of these signposts. I lost my balance and fell. According to my standards, stumbling over a curb or missing a step in an awkward way is bad, but falling is inexcusable. If I had to fall, why did it have to be on a day when so many important people were around?

My first thought was, "Who saw me?" I soon found out that at least one person did.

"Oh, here. Let me help you up." His voice was kind enough, perhaps too kind. "Are you hurt?"

I didn't recognize the voice and I wondered who he was, but first things first. "No, I'm all right. Only my pride has been hurt. Boy, I hope my blind students don't hear about this." I always insisted that they use proper cane techniques wherever they went.

I was on my feet now, brushing the dirt off my clothes.

"Are you sure you're okay now?" my new friend asked. "I'll walk you to your room, if you like."

"Thanks, but I'm fine." I asked who he was. He was with a company who hired a lot of our graduates. I left it at that, glad the embarrassing episode was over.

I mentioned the incident to a few of my teacher friends but not to any of my students. A few days later, though, I discovered that the man who offered to help me was not the only one who saw me fall. One of my students approached me about the matter.

"Yes, I fell," I said. I admitted that I was not using my cane in the proper way. I tried to point out that even in such a situation a person must try to conduct himself with dignity. As I expounded on how this kind of thing can happen to anyone, I suddenly realized that what I was saying to my student, I should have been saying to myself.

The real climax to the incident came two weeks later when another of my students brought up the subject. He had been listening to the radio and had heard that some blind lady who taught at the Vocational School had fallen. I did a double take and had him repeat everything he had said.

"Was it you, Debby?" his voice was understanding, but he really did want to know.

"Yes, it was," I replied quietly. "It happened the day all those important people were here."

But why on the radio? I found out later that the public hearing had been recorded and was broadcast a few weeks later. The man who had seen me fall had made favorable reference to the experience publicly. I think his point was something about the dedication of the faculty at our school. I'm not sure.

I do know that I learned a lot through it all. No one around me thought that my fall was something of which I should be ashamed or embarrassed. Why should I waste good time worrying about it when I could put the same mental energy to better use?

Blind persons often find themselves in awkward situations. Some tend to demand perfection of themselves. Others may react in the opposite way and hardly even try. Without proper sensory and mobility training, a blind person may come to feel that he can never achieve dignity. He may then use his blindness as an excuse for lack of poise, sloppy dress, bad table manners, and practically no social skills. It is easy for him to forget that he can compete with the sighted world in all these areas, although he may need to make some allowances here and there.

The two extremes of ultrasensitivity about mistakes and not caring at all can be equally dangerous. The happy medium is striving for poise and awareness, keeping in mind that if this cannot be achieved in every situation, all is not lost.

When I discovered that my friends did not insist on impossibly high standards of behavior, I relaxed. They too could relax, knowing that if a bad situation arose we could laugh about it together. I became less sensitive about accepting help from others and more open about discussing my problems with them. I found that those around me would gladly help me much more than they did. Not knowing how to help was one obstacle. But realizing I might interpret their offer to help as an insult had kept them from extending a hand when I needed it.

I was grateful for the new insights I received through the embarrassment of falling that day. But there were more experiences still ahead of me that would teach me other important lessons.

Bruised Shins

Bruised Shins

RECENTLY I read a book on body language. It explained how different body positions and glances carry a wide variety of meanings. I became aware how crucial eye contact is for communicating effectively with others. Perhaps this is why some people find conversation with a blind person disconcerting. Little or no eye contact can be just as devastating to good communication as a glance that lingers a bit too long.

Although I have one prosthesis (artificial eye) and the vision in my other eye is almost nil, I always try to look directly at a person when I talk. I look where his eyes should be in relation to the sound of his voice. Sometimes this works out well. But sometimes the other person is wearing soft-soled shoes or standing on carpet and moving quietly from one spot to another while I'm talking to him. It gets to be quite funny. I'm trying hard to focus on where I think his face should be, based on his voice the last time he spoke. But when he responds, I discover that he has moved two feet to the right and I have been talking to the wall.

I am glad my friends have learned to live with this kind of poor eye contact. Occasionally, I feel uneasy because people are able to look into my eyes. Aren't eyes the windows to the soul? I wonder if they can see things in my face and eyes that I would rather keep to myself. At those times I lower or turn my head to keep them from seeing more than I would like them to see.

Lack of eye contact is not the only area of body communication that can easily be misinterpreted. A simple thing like shaking hands may make the blind person seem cold and unfriendly when the problem is simply that he doesn't see the extended hand. At the Airport Gardens Baptist Church in Hazard, where I am a member, we do a lot of handshaking. When new members join the church or rededicate their lives to God, the minister asks the people to come to the front of the church, shake hands with the persons who have made the new commitment, and then return to their seats. Most of the time, I do not participate. This isn't because I do not wish these friends well, but the technical problems seem overwhelming.

One day I was getting my hair done in a shop at the Vocational School. My hair had been cut, washed, set, and was now drying. With the dryer humming in my ears, I could hear nothing of what was going on around me in the room. Later that day, a friend asked me if I always slept under the dryer.

"I wasn't sleeping," I said defensively.

"Then you're getting pretty stuck up," she said, "I walked right by you and waved and you never noticed." She stopped. Then she laughed and added, "Debby, would you believe that I just now realized why you didn't wave back to me?"

I thanked her for the compliment. It felt good to be thought of as an average sort of individual and not as a poor blind person.

Forgetting a person's blindness is not, unfortunately, common. When it happens to me, I usually consider it a compliment. However, it does have its disadvantages. While visiting with a friend in Lexington, Kentucky, he and I were looking around in some of the big department stores. He had just informed me that if he forgot to tell me about a step, it was because he kept forgetting that I am blind. I had hold of his arm so I could usually tell when he went up or down a step. I had my cane but wasn't using it as we walked through the store. He kept forgetting all right. I collected a few bruise marks on my right leg from his turning corners too short. He kept thinking I would see the narrow aisle and walked behind him. We had some good laughs over that.

Just how much help a blind person wants or needs and what kind of help would benefit the most can vary. When I first had my cane, I believed that I could do practically everything myself. I wanted others to think so also. I'd ask for help only of a close friend and in the most private situations. Many times I needed help, but I didn't want it.

This became apparent to me one day in the school

cafeteria. A colleague from Rehabilitation Services and I were having lunch together. The meat was particularly difficult to handle that day. I usually have no trouble with meat but this piece was tough.

Observing my struggle for a while, my friend finally spoke up. "Debby, I'll cut that meat off for you if you like," he said in a genuine tone without a bit of condescension. But I refused his kindness.

"Thanks, Larry, but if I can't cut the meat from the bone myself, I don't want to eat it."

"That's a lot of good food to let go to waste," he chided. "I'd be glad to help you."

But I felt my ego was at stake. I still refused. I managed to cut a little meat off the bone and threw the rest away. I tried to analyze why I hadn't found it possible to let him help me with a simple task when I obviously needed assistance.

Living independently is an art. But gradually I came to realize that accepting help when it is needed is a much finer art. And I have learned that even this can be done gracefully, with no loss of dignity.

When I first started working at the Vocational School, they assigned a fellow named Harv to drive me to various places in the county to contact people who might be interested in our program for the blind. I wanted to do as much as I could myself without becoming a burden to him.

Harv was kind and understanding. He let me do things my way. I realize now how much easier it would have been for both of us if I had taken the arm he offered as we climbed up and down the sides of those hills. He gave me excellent verbal directions, though, and we made it with no fatalities.

Recently Harv and I were at the same conference. As we were leaving with some others, it was necessary for us to walk through a room where another meeting was still in session. The contrast in my attitude surprised both Harv and me. "How about an arm, Harv, till we get outside," I ventured.

I could have walked through the room alone or by following someone's verbal directions. But using my cane would have been quite disruptive.

I have learned that accepting help need not be threatening to one's ego. I used to feel that a person who offered to help me thought he was better than I. In most cases this is not true. Since I discovered that people are genuinely interested in helping me as a person, I am much more likely to ask for help. And when these same people allow me to do something for them in return, the circle is completed and I know I am not inferior in their eyes.

There are those, however, who do offer assistance in a condescending way. Accepting help of this kind gracefully is difficult but even more important. Negative or childish behavior only serves to strengthen what they already suspect.

I like it when people are sensitive and kind when they offer to help me. I like it when they offer assistance not because it's "Be Kind to Blind People Week" or because they're Boy Scouts working on their Good Samaritan badges, but because I'm a person and they want to show they care. I like it when they respect my occasional decision to refuse their help, and when they remember that each time I am offered assistance, the battle of independence versus graceful coexistence with my fellowman starts up again.

Perhaps this problem area is not unique to blind people. Fear of the unknown is common to us all. But being blind, I struggled with many unknowns.

A Mouse in the Bathtub

A Mouse in the Bathtub

THE SUMMER before my last semester of college and the year before I started work at the Hazard Vocational School, I was teaching braille in Hyden with the Summer Appalachia Seminar. Another girl and I were staying together in a large old house. We shared the same bedroom, ate our meals in the kitchen, and used another of the rooms for my classes.

It had stood empty for part of the year. Mice, and I suppose rats, had made themselves at home in it. We never saw any, but mornings while I was in the bathroom, I could hear them running in the walls. I had no fear of mice at that point. In fact, I would tap on the wall with my finger to hear them run some more. It became sort of a game with me. Then one morning it happened.

I got up early, as I usually do. I walked into the bathroom, disrobed, and turned on the tub water for a morning bath. That's when I heard it — a sound identical to the ones I had been hearing in the wall. But this time it was not in the wall. It was much closer than that. Realizing that the mouse must be in the bathroom, I opened the door to let him out. The sound of pitter-pattering feet continued. Where was he? Finally, I decided the mouse was in the tub. The hot water was probably forcing the mouse to try to climb up the slippery back of the tub. But the water was running out almost as fast as it ran in because I failed to put in the plug.

I was scared stiff. I stood in the center of the bathroom, still unclothed, afraid to move. If I could have known for sure that the mouse was actually in the tub, I think half my fear would have been gone. But I didn't know for sure, and in those moments a phobia was born.

I slowly recovered most of my composure but not enough to bend over and turn off the bath water. I tried to put on my hairpiece, but dropped a bobby pin on the floor. I was too terrified to pick it up; I just reached for another one. I dressed and left the bathroom with the water still running. Soon the cook who fixed food for my students arrived. I asked her to see if there was a mouse in the tub.

She looked, turned off the water, and the sound stopped. "No, Debby, there's no mouse here," she assured me. "Did you think you heard one?"

"Yes, I did," was all I could manage to say. After she left, I turned the water back on, but nothing sounded like tiny feet running. I decided some air must have been caught in the pipe causing the eerie sound. I tried to forget it, but a fear of mice was now a part of me.

Almost a year later when I rented the room in Hazard, Kentucky, and was teaching, this fear of mice and rats remained with me. Fortunately, though, I had no real encounters with any of these furry creatures while I was living alone.

During my stay there, I met a friend who was also of Mennonite background. Myrna Miller, a nurse at the Hazard Hospital, had an apartment and was living alone. When I returned from my month of vacation in July, I moved in with her.

Before Myrna rented the apartment, it had stood empty several months. During this time, some desperate river rats had taken advantage of the situation. By the time I moved in, Myrna had the rat problem well under control and she assured me she hadn't seen one for several weeks. I was still a bit uneasy. She was working evenings; so most of the time I was alone in the apartment and my imagination would run wild. I appreciated the wall-to-wall carpet on the floor but was also aware that if a rat or a mouse ran across the floor, I likely wouldn't hear it. I didn't want a hateful rodent to be in the room with me, but if one was, I wanted to know about it.

Once when Myrna and I were sitting at the kitchen table, we heard a scratching noise.

"Did you hear that, Debby?" Myrna asked. "It sounds like a mouse. I think it's behind the refrigerator." Myrna was supercalm about things like that, but for some reason her calmness did not rub off on me.

She set a trap, which my sister had given to me for Christmas that year as a joke, and caught the mouse.

We had to use the trap several other times. Every time I thought I had my phobia under control, another mouse would appear on the scene and I would have to start the process all over again.

One evening when I was alone in the apartment, my sister Donna called me from Eastern Mennonite College at Harrisonburg, Virginia. She just wanted to find out how things were going with me. We were in the middle of discussing the kinds of things sisters talk about, when I heard a sound that froze me. Tiny feet were scratching or running or something. There was no point in trying to hide my fear from Donna.

"Donna, I hear something. I think a mouse is running around in this room. I'm scared."

She tried to reassure me. "Well, Debby, if it's a mouse, it's probably running away from you. Listen, can you still hear it?"

I listened. Yes, I could hear it but there was something strange about it. The sound was not coming from the floor but from somewhere over my head. I stomped my foot a time or two but the persistent creature kept right on with whatever it was he was doing. I managed to bring my imagination under control and reassured Donna that all would be fine. After we finished our conversation, I could no longer hear the strange sound and within a few days almost forgot about it.

Not quite, though. Through my work at the school, I came to know and respect a Mr. Paul Collins who worked in job placement for Rehabilitation Services. We did some publicity work together and his advice and guidance were invaluable to me. I told him about my fear of mice and rats. One evening we were at the apartment doing some planning when suddenly, with no warning at all, I heard that strange sound again. As before, I froze. But this time I was not alone.

"Sh," I whispered. "Do you hear that?"

He listened. "Yes, I hear it."

"What is it? Where is it coming from?"

He got to his feet and walked over to the wall. The sound seemed to be coming from directly above him. He stood still and listened. I stayed where I was, too frightened to move.

"What do you think it is?" I interrupted the silence.

"Whatever it is," he hedged, "it's on the outside. It must be something that came in under the eaves. This is the outside wall. Evidently there's a hole on the outside through which something got in the space above the ceiling."

If I was supposed to be relieved by that explanation, I wasn't. Paul sensed that I was still scared and came over and sat down. His years of counseling as a minister and his education served him well as he tried to calm my fears.

"Now, listen, Debby," he began. "I don't know what's up there. It might be a mouse. But then, again, it might be a bird. I can't tell. I do know his name, though."

"How could you?" I asked doubtfully. "What is it?"

"Amicus," he replied mischievously. "Do you remember what that means from your Latin days?"

"Yes, it means 'friend.' "

"Right. Now Amicus is wanting to move in up there

and he has quite a bit to do. He's working as fast as he can. He knows that the sound of feet scares you, but there's nothing he can do about that. All he knows to do is work as fast as he can so you'll have less time to be frightened. He also knows that I'm here with you and that you'll not be quite so terrified as if he did his work when you were alone."

He was talking to me as if I were a child, but as he elaborated on how bad Amicus felt about scaring me when he had no intentions of harming anyone, I began to see how really childish my fear was.

"Now if you'll just decide that you enjoy having him around, he'll be able to work much better," Paul continued. "Look at it this way. Amicus is here to keep you company. Isn't it good to know that when he has finished moving in, you won't ever be alone? He'll be here when you get home from work and he'll keep you company all evening."

I was laughing by now. "It's really silly to be scared of a little animal, isn't it?" I queried, expecting agreement.

"No, sometimes you need to fear things for your own protection. But it is silly to be afraid of Amicus."

The idea took hold. Soon I came to enjoy the scratching sound and missed it when Amicus was out for the evening. We never learned for sure just who Amicus was. I like to think he was a bird, although, as it turned out, he'd have been just as welcome if he had been a mouse.

I told my family about Amicus. But still I was surprised one day to receive a long-distance telephone call from Uncle Ellrose and have him ask, "May I speak with

Mr. Amicus?" We both laughed.

Though I have no overwhelming urge to find a mouse and pet it, I am no longer terror-stricken when I think one may be close. I've tried not to let the crippling demon of fear control me in any area of my life.

As I learned through my experiences with mice, many fears are ungrounded. Although this is true for everyone, it is an insight of special significance for those who are blind.

From Rocks to Stepping-Stones

From Rocks to Stepping-Stones

IN ALL MY experiences God has been present even though the nature of that presence has varied from time to time.

During one of my summers in college, I decided to try to take a few courses that I had missed while out of school learning braille. Instead of enrolling at Juniata College, where I attended during the winter months, I registered for two biology courses at the nearest state school. This was Shippensburg State College, about thirty miles from home. I commuted each day.

Before the first class, my mother and I went to the campus. We spoke with the professor, telling him of my disability and how I planned to work around it with textbooks on tape and braille class notes. We also made arrangements for taking tests. Then my mother

113

helped acquaint me with the layout of the campus. We located the room where I would be having my classes, the cafeteria, and other buildings with which I should be acquainted. I was off to a good start.

Since the professor obviously had never taught a blind person before, minor problems arose from time to time. But we managed to work our way through them successfully. The other members of the small class seemed intrigued by my learning methods. One classmate even improvised a learning aid for me. We were studying the circulatory system of a frog. She drew the diagram of this system on typing paper, then painstakingly outlined the arteries with red yarn to represent the freshness of the blood as it flowed away from the heart. The veins carrying the blood back to the heart and lungs, she indicated with thin wire. It must have taken her a long time and I shall always be indebted to her for my knowledge of the frog's circulatory system. I thank God for her.

The first summer term ended and the second began. I had registered for my second-term work at the beginning of the summer, but discovered it would be necessary to register again for the second term. It was a Monday morning and my mother was in Mount Union totally unaware of my predicament. If you've ever struggled through the confusion of college registration lines, you have some idea why I was a bit apprehensive as I walked slowly toward the college gym. It would be filled with a maze of tables and a crush of people.

Really, the registration operation was well organized. One merely walked up to the first desk, gave the lady behind it the information she needed, accepted the papers she handed you, filled them out, and returned them to the table she indicated. The tables were all numbered and the route through the gym would depend on one's classification as a student.

Walking to the first table, answering her questions, and taking the papers she offered presented no problem. She indicated a table at the side which had been designated for filling out papers. I went to the table and sat down. I was not at all sure what I was going to do next.

How would God help me solve the problem of filling out these forms? Up to this point in my experience of trusting God, He had always provided help for me when I needed it — sometimes in the most interesting ways. On the Juniata campus, we girls would make regular trips to the grocery store several blocks away. We'd buy snack foods to take to our rooms, and pick up personal items such as hose. More than once I'd gone alone and located the various items I needed with no major problem. The different sizes and shapes of the packages helped me identify them. But to select the style and color of panty hose I wanted was a more difficult matter. I could distinguish between regular hose and panty hose easily enough because of the thickness of the package. But how was I to find the right size and shade? That was the kind of situation where God showed His love and power over and over again.

"God, I'd like a small size in a medium dark shade."

Then I would stand in front of the rack and flip through the packages with my fingers. When one of the packages seemed to stand out, I'd pick it up and take it with me. I never got anything I didn't want.

But the problem of filling out a registration form seemed different. I hoped God didn't mind my depending on Him to get me through a jam like this, but I didn't think I had much choice.

"Hey, God," I prayed silently, "You see this form here. I have to fill it out and take it to table four. You know I can't see to fill it out and I have no idea where table four is. I guess I am going to have to ask You again to help me through this one."

Then I sat and waited. And I didn't feel silly. I knew He would come to my rescue. I had no idea how, though, and I was anxious to find out.

I don't know how long I sat there. Other students came, sat down, filled out their forms, and left. The hustle and bustle coming from all over the huge room continued, and still I waited.

A timid voice from across the table finally broke through the din. "Excuse me. Is your name Debby?"

"Yes, it is." I looked up, but the voice was unfamiliar to me.

"Would you like me to fill out those forms for you?" It was the voice of an angel sent from my God.

"That would surely be nice." I responded. "But who are you?"

She told me. I had been introduced to her a few days earlier. She was a friend of one of the girls in my biology class. But still she was my angel.

She was taking summer work at this college with the hope of transferring the credits to another school. The school she attended regularly was one with a Christian emphasis. I explained to her why I was just sitting there the way I was and how I was depending on God to provide the help I needed. "You're my special angel," I concluded.

She laughed, but understood. Since we were both summer students, our route through the gym was identical. God certainly is good. He hadn't let me down.

The way He demonstrates His goodness in my life has varied a great deal. For my last semester on the Juniata campus, I had the opportunity of living in a new coed dormitory. Men and women lived in the same building, though not on the same floor. We didn't have much trouble putting up with that. But we did complain about the distance the dorm was located from the rest of the campus. According to my calculations, based on the number of steps around the football field, it was exactly a quarter of a mile. The walkways were good, though not quite finished, when we moved in that fall. A little creek ran in front of the dorm and the walk which went over it was adequate except for one thing. The railing on the sides hadn't been installed yet.

This was no problem for most of the students, but my friends seemed a bit apprehensive about my safety. I could usually see the sidewalk because of its color contrast from the surrounding grass. Occasionally, though, if the light was not right or the wet rain made the sidewalk a darker color, I would have some trouble. I might step off it. On a regular sidewalk, I'd simply step back on it again. But if I went off the side of the bridge, things would not have been so simple to remedy.

I managed. God was always with me and guided my steps. Within a few months I was learning to use a cane at the Greater Pittsburgh Guild for the Blind. It was no longer necessary for me to depend on God for some of the details of finding my way around. With proper use, my cane would indicate the edge of sidewalks and bridges. I learned that the way to select items like hosiery, where size and shape of the package were of no help, was to learn the usual location of the item on the shelf in relation to some fixed object. If that didn't work, I was told, I should not hesitate to ask a store employee for assistance.

One day I was discussing the benefits of this training with a friend who was aware of how I had relied on God to keep me walking straight. "But you know," I concluded, "with this cane, I don't have to depend on God."

My friend was horrified. "Don't you ever say that. Just because you can walk around safely now doesn't mean you no longer need God."

"Did I say that? I didn't mean even to imply it," I replied. "The areas of dependence have changed, that's all."

My trust in God has continued and has grown. I look to Him to keep me on the right path in life and to show me new areas to explore. With Him, I can successfully bypass dangerous obstacles, turning the rocks in my path into useful stepping-stones.

God Loves and Understands

God Loves and Understands

ONE NEVER knows where a path may lead. At times it may look as though it doesn't lead anywhere. But when a Christian walks with his Master, the path leads one closer to Him.

Sometimes events in my life seem to have little immediate influence on my spiritual growth. But a subtle effect is often there just the same. I recall the course in American literature I took at Juniata College. Students are required to take some electives in addition to the courses in the area of their major. This provides a well-rounded education and hopefully a balanced person. My major was sociology and this literature course was one of my electives. We were reading works from early American writers — Emerson, Thoreau, Dickinson, Melbourne, and Whitman.

I was pleasantly surprised to discover the spiritual depth of Emerson and the earthiness of Thoreau. Dickinson was delightful. But when we came to Whitman, I almost cringed. His subject matter was so common. I was having trouble appreciating his works as I thought I should, and couldn't quite understand why.

It became clear one day when I stopped in my professor's office to check an assignment that I didn't understand completely.

"So how are things going?" he asked after we had resolved the immediate problem.

"Oh, fine, I guess," I responded. "But I'm having a hard time with Walt. I'm not sure why."

He thought a moment, then turned and reached for something on his desk. "Take this," he said.

He was handing me an object. I reached for it and ran my fingers over it.

"Can you tell what it is?"

"It looks like a foot," I ventured. It seemed to be a miniature wax foot about three inches long.

"You're right," he said. "But that's not all. Here look at this." He indicated something at the ankle of the foot.

I checked and discovered a wick. So it was a candle.

He saw the questioning look on my face.

"Oh, I get it," I replied after a few moments of reflection. "The candle represents idealism, yet it's in the shape of a foot — a common, down-to-earth foot." From that day to this I have been better able to understand Whitman's way of writing.

I recall another experience that helped me to deeper spiritual understandings. Because of my determination to be aware of the needs of people around me, I became involved in a sensitivity training weekend.

The purpose of this retreat was to consider what human interaction is all about. A man trained in this field accompanied a group of about twelve of us, of various ages and walks of life, to a country home for a weekend. Most of us were total strangers to each other. We were all uneasy on Friday night as we gathered in the living room of the huge home.

We talked about why each of us had come, trying to be honest. We discussed the games people play in their dealings with each other. We tried to understand why people react as they do. We shared our good points and our weaknesses. By Sunday afternoon, as we were preparing to leave, we felt a closeness that I would have thought impossible. We all hated to part.

Most of the members of that group, I have never seen again. But I learned a lot. Although the weekend had no direct spiritual emphasis, I felt my God at work, teaching me more things about Himself. I realized that the kind of rapport we strangers experienced with each other is the kind of involvement most of us long for. If it was possible for us to achieve this closeness in spite of our different ideas and attitudes about God, why does the church, where love is supreme, have so much trouble running smoothly? I concluded that if the people who make up the church really cared deeply for each other, the gimmicks we use to try to get people to come to church would be unnecessary. The church would be filled with those who sense the warmth there and want to be a part of it.

I have found that God uses a wide variety of situations to teach His children. When we ask Him, He pulls us close to Himself, though we may not understand the way He works. In this day of renewed interest in spiritual things, the Spirit of God is plainly at work. We long to be where the action is, but all too often we only know about it from books and magazine articles. We read of thousands being reached for Christ and rejoice. Churches that once were dead are becoming alive. Lukewarm Christians are making new commitments. In prayer, we feel God's Spirit and praise Him for His love.

But questions go unanswered. I have never been bitter toward God, but I have wondered why I remain without sight while others around me experience God's healing touch.

When I am told that faith is all that is required, I conclude that my faith is too small. But I receive answers to my other prayers. Someone else tells me that I can be healed only if it is God's will. But then another of His children comes along and tries to convince me that sickness and imperfection are never His will. Others tell me to keep my thoughts health-centered, not even to think of imperfection and disease. Still others advise me to pray for healing and accept it as accomplished. They tell me I'm trying too hard, that I should simply let God do it.

I am grateful for well-intentioned advice, but I'm even more grateful for the genuine love and concern shown by friends.

One day I was made aware of a pitfall in seeking physical healing. I observed a friend on this quest. It was obvious to me that she was focusing her entire life and all her energies toward this goal. In all of her efforts, she was clearly miserable and missing out on life.

I'm glad my God is not only powerful, but that He also understands me. I have asked for His presence in my life and have yielded all to Him. If something is wrong with my attitude, or if my faith is insufficient, or if sight is not part of His will, I rest assured that He is aware of that and can bring me to the point I need to be. In the meantime, I do not intend to miss out on the fullness of life available to me.

I have discovered the joy of gratitude. I have experienced the thrill of trusting in His divine plan. It is not necessary that I understand what will come tomorrow or why. Is it not enough that He loves me and is powerful enough to mold me into the person He means for me to be?

I am learning to be content with the things that I can do nothing about. I rest on the knowledge that He is working out His perfect will in my life. The songwriter put it well:

And when His will, I do not understand,
I can pray, "Do not let go my hand."

Wanting to live in His will and accepting physical handicaps are good. But the ability to be grateful for these limitations even when we can't see how they could benefit us, or those around us, is an important next step. Eugenia Price talks of drinking deeply of life. Sometimes when we put the cup of life to our lips, it may be sweet and we can drink deeply without difficulty. In other situations, though, we find a bitter taste as we raise the cup to our lips. Then, too, we must drink the contents, not only willingly, but deeply and gratefully.

Part of the truth that makes us free is our knowledge as Christians that God's limitless love surrounds us, no matter how dark our lot may seem. Faith in ultimate good being achieved frees us to live in the light and to experience life to the full.

THE AUTHOR

Deborah Zook was born in Mt. Union, Pa. She lost the sight of one eye at the age of eight. In spite of medical and surgical efforts to help her, she gradually lost the sight in her other eye.

Debby graduated from the Mt. Union High School in 1966 and received her BA degree in sociology from Juniata College, Huntingdon, Pa., in 1971. She graduated from the Greater Pittsburgh Guild for the Blind, Bridgeville, Pa., in the spring of 1971.

After completing her training at the Guild, Debby be-